101 Ways to Teach and Entertain Your Toddler

Activities and Games for Every Season!

Sophia Lawson

ISBN-13: 978-1482586510
ISBN-10: 1482586517

Disclaimer: Supervise young children at all times, and use your best judgment when choosing activities which are safe and appropriate for your child's readiness level, particularly when the activity involves water hazards or potential for choking. Information included in this book has been compiled from numerous sources and is of a general nature only and must not be relied upon in substitution for professional advice. While all attempts have been made to provide effective, verifiable information in this book, neither the author nor publisher assumes responsibility for errors, inaccuracies or omissions. Any slights of people or organizations are unintentional. This book is not a source of medical information. This book shall not be copied or distributed without expressed permission from the publisher.

Dedication

Thanks and acknowledgement goes to all the creative mothers, experts and friends who helped brainstorm and contribute to this book. Many thanks to my daughter for inspiring me to create new games and activities to keep your mind and body engaged. Last but not least, thank you to my husband for your endless encouragement and support.

CONTENTS

TEACHING AND ENTERTAINING YOUR TODDLER

Do you ever feel like you are going through the motions, following the same play routines every day? Possibly throwing in an outing or two, but wondering if your toddler is really learning and experiencing all that he could? You are not alone! Many parents find themselves out of ideas or options for keeping their toddler's curiosity and mind peaked day after day.

This book is a compilation of some of the best ideas to give parents inspiration and tips for entertaining and teaching your precious little one in every season of the year! All the activities will work with boys or girls, though there are also ideas included that are extra fun for boys or super sweet for girls. Some of the ideas are extremely simple, while others involve a bit more craftiness and planning. Plus, this book isn't just a top 100 list; it includes recipes, craft instructions, game how-to's, detailed activity explanations, and more.

A Passion for Playtime

It's a familiar scene. Your active, curious little one makes his way over to the bookshelf and begins pulling the books and magazines into a pile on the floor. Is his attention occupied? Yes. But is he learning or engaging with his senses? Not quite. And as a busy parent, you shouldn't fret. This is normal, and it's okay. But you also know that play is a vital part of your child's social, emotional, physical and mental development. Your little one will fine-tune the use of his five senses during these critical years. Exploration is a driving force, and your baby or toddler will watch, touch, taste, and listen to his surroundings, not to mention test what is acceptable or unacceptable in this big world. Playing isn't just your little one's way of biding time; it's his passion and primary purpose during these early years.

Throughout the first year of life, your baby learns and grows, gaining more mobility every month. Then as your baby passes his 1-year birthday, his world expands tremendously. Play time becomes increasingly imaginative and complex. He'll begin problem solving and expanding his independence and creativity. With increased mobility and curiosity comes the urgency from Mom and Dad to keep your child engaged, entertained and out of trouble. While keeping your child occupied and safe are important for every parent, the possibilities for your toddler to learn and grow are also tremendous.

Trash Becomes Treasure

The toys available today are wonderful, and there are practically countless options. Less expensive consignment shops are also widely available and are full of toys and books that can find new life with a battery and disinfectant wipe. Though toys are a wonderful option, you don't need to spend a lot of money to keep your toddler engaged. There are many basic items and ideas that cost little to no money, and are often found in your home.

A child can learn and play with so many different objects – items that your family probably uses every day. For little ones, trash becomes treasure. As you finish using certain objects like cereal boxes, butter tubs, paper bags, paper towel rolls, and more, save them (and wash if necessary) for future use in a project. Paired with a few basic craft supplies (like pom balls, yarn or pipe cleaners), these items can be used for fun later on.

Before You Begin

As always, please supervise your child and take caution if the items or environments pose a risk depending on your child's age or development.

Enjoy uncovering the ideas and inspiration in this book, and above all, encourage the passion for play in your precious toddler!

Sophia Lawson

CHAPTER 1

AREAS OF DEVELOPMENT & TYPES OF PLAY

As you think about the ideas and inspiration listed in this book, consider the activities in the context of the vital areas of development.

Areas of Development

- **Fine Motor:** The coordination of small muscle movements occurring in body parts such as the fingers, usually in coordination with the eyes (as in hand-eye coordination).

- **Gross Motor:** Bigger movements of the body in coordination with the mind which engage the large muscles in the arms, legs, feet and torso.

- **Communication:** The ability to use language and express behavior so that information is successfully passed along, received and understood.

- **Personal-Social:** Communicating, relating to, and socializing with others in a healthy manner.

- **Problem Solving:** Using critical thinking and working through the details of an issue, in an orderly manner, to find a solution.

Types of Play

As your toddler grows, he should engage in age-appropriate activities that ultimately span all the areas of play to ensure well-rounded social, emotional, physical and mental development.

Object play

From 4 to 10 months and beyond, touching, banging, tossing, pushing and experimenting with objects is fascinating and fun.

Social play

The first year may be filled with smiling, laughing or following an object with the eyes. Older babies will begin to enjoy basic games like itsy-bitsy-spider, peek-a-boo, "so big," or patty-cake. Toddlers will begin sharing with you or playing games with other children. No matter the age, interacting with you, and then others, is important.

Functional and representational play

Pretending or trying to use every day objects in an appropriate way encourages the imagination and basic skills for your toddler, such as: pushing a toy lawn mower or grocery cart, brushing hair, trying to put on a sock or pretending to make a call with a phone. It's wonderful to see little imaginations come to life!

Early symbolic play

Around the age of 2, your toddler begins to create something out of nothing, perhaps with a soundtrack as they act along. Examples are play eating or making a car out of a box while saying "vroom!"

Role play

Break out the costumes! Your little princess or action hero will begin acting out roles around 30 to 36 months. You might see them playing doctor, pretending to teach a teddy bear, or "being mommy" as they mimic you folding the laundry.

Now that we've discussed the essential areas of development and types of play, let's get to the ultimate list of games and activities for your toddler! Enjoy!

Sophia Lawson

CHAPTER 2

WINTER ACTIVITIES

Celebrating the holidays and a new year creates opportunity for fun, while being stuck indoors requires some extra creativity.

1. Tub painting

This is a perfect activity for winter because it allows your child to get messy, use water and make art – all indoors away from the cold. Put your child in the tub either unclothed or in a bathing suit. Give your child washable finger paint or water colors and a paintbrush or sponge; or they can also simply use their hands.

When they are done painting on the tub walls, simply wash away.

2. Make a felt Christmas tree

This is a no-sew project that will provide entertainment throughout the holiday season. You'll need ¾ yard of 72" green felt, about four small sheets of various colored felt, Heat'n Bond sheets, a few Command™ picture-hanging strips, scissors and an iron.

Lightly trace a tree on the back of the felt and cut it out. Hang your tree on a wall using the Command strips for easy removal later on.

Next, cut ornament bases out of a few of the other felt sheets. Then trace out decorations (stripes, letters, numbers, etc.) onto the paper side of the Heat'n Bond sheets. Cut just outside the traced line, and iron the paper shapes onto your desired felt colors. Cut the felt directly along the traced line and peel off the paper backing. Place the decorations on your ornament base, and iron into place.

Now, your child can decorate their very own Christmas tree. Because felt sticks naturally to felt, the ornaments will stay on your tree but will remove easily for redecorating all season long.

3. Stamping

Grab an ink pad, paper and a variety of stamps and let your toddler create a picture. Create your own stamps with foam sheets by letting your toddler cut out shapes, and then glue the foam to the lid from a baby food jar or coffee can.

4. Color scavenger hunt

Give your child a paper bag with a color scribbled on the front and ask them to run around the house until they find items of that color to put in the bag. Limit the search to child-friendly rooms and consider rigging the search with a few items ahead of time. Give your child 10 minutes to search for items, then reconvene in the living room to explore his treasures.

5. Make a magazine face

Magazines can be fun for younger toddlers, who will flip through the pages and point at objects or rip them out all together. Older toddlers can take magazine fun one step further by making a game out of finding objects. One variation is to make a magazine face. Ask them to find a picture they like of eyes, ears, nose, smile, and hair. Help them cut out their favorite items and they can arrange one or two magazine faces. They can interchange the features to change how the face looks.

6. Gingerbread dice game

On a plain sheet of paper, draw a large outline of a Gingerbread Man. Divide the man into 12 sections, and write a number in each section (1 – 12). Then, write the numbers 1 – 12 on scraps of paper and place them in a container. Shake up the numbers and have your toddler draw a number. Your toddler will then color in the section of the number that he has drawn. Keep going until the Gingerbread Man is colored in completely. You can also play this game with dice instead of pieces of paper. This game helps your toddler learn to identify numbers and begin to understand the very basic levels of math.

7. Push pom-pom balls

Cut small holes (slightly smaller than your poms) into the lid of a butter tub (or similar object). Use multiple colored pom balls, which are found at any craft store. Have your toddler push the poms through the holes. For extra brain power for older children, color the rims of the holes to match the colors of the poms, and have your child push the poms through the matching colored holes.

8. Have fun with music

If you own pretend musical instruments, break them out. But if not, pots and pans and giant spoons work great. Put on some music, bang on a drum and dance around with your little one. Any type of music will do! For one toddler favorite, try out the Toddler Station on Pandora radio (www.pandora.com).

For a fun music game, play "Freeze!" Simply start up the music and dance around. When Mommy hits "pause" on the CD/computer your toddler must freeze until the music starts again. Very young toddlers may only be amused by this for a few minutes, but older toddlers could play this game over and over again.

9. New Year's Eve countdown bags

Whether you are watching the ball drop at home with your little one or heading out to have some fun while the babysitter takes over for the night, get your toddler involved in the New Year's Eve festivities with this fun activity. Make countdown bags by decorating the outside of each bag with the hour they may open it (6 p.m., 7 p.m., and so on). Fill the inside of the bag with a treat or special game they can play when they open it. For example, lead older children on a scavenger hunt for party poppers, or entertain your little one with colorful glittery pom balls. If they aren't old enough to stay up until midnight, have the bags lead up until their bedtime and proclaim it New Year's.

10. Make snowflake art

Pick up a small canvas from your craft store. Hobby Lobby is a great go-to because they typically have a 40%-off printable coupon on their website (www.hobbylobby.com), which makes a single canvas very affordable. This will also work if you use a thick piece of paper. Crisscross painters tape on the canvas or paper in a snowflake design. Give your little painter water color and a brush or sponge and let them do whatever they like to the canvas. At the end, peel off the tape, and they've created their very on snowflake art!

11. Make a texture fun zone

Purchase or recycle a large cookie sheet to create a texture fun zone for your toddler. A popular location for these boards is the kitchen where your toddler can learn and entertain himself while you're cooking or cleaning. This board will serve as a teaching tool to understand various textures, cause and effect, the alphabet, numbers, shapes, and more.

What you'll need:

A large metal cookie sheet

Velcro

Felt (at least two colors)

Chalkboard paint and chalk

Magnet toys (letters, numbers, etc.)

Command picture hanging strips

Hot glue gun

Ribbon (optional)

Board instructions: Section four areas of your cookie sheet for each "texture": Velcro, magnets, felt and chalkboard. This can be done in exact squares or randomly based on your preference. Apply the chalkboard paint in the first area of the board. Hot glue one color of your felt in the second area. Hot glue the soft side of the Velcro to the board in the third area. Leave the fourth area blank. Embellish the edges of the cookie sheet if you want extra pizzazz. Position the Command strips on the back of the sheet and mount the sheet in the location of your choice, such as on a wall or a door.

Accessory instructions: In the blank section, place magnets for your child to play with. Alphabet letters or numbers are a great choice. For the Velcro section, hot glue the scratchy side of your Velcro onto the items of your choice, and stick them up on the board. For the felt area, cut shapes or animals out of the other colored felt, and stick them on the board (felt sticks to felt). Finally, in the chalkboard section, you'll want to supply chalk for drawing. If your toddler is old enough to have total access to chalk, affix a piece of chalk to the board by hot gluing a ribbon to the back of the board and tying the other end around the piece of chalk so that it hangs by the board. However, younger toddlers may try to eat the chalk, so use caution. Keep the chalk tucked away and pull it out for playtime when you can closely supervise.

12. Holiday sensory bin

Create a holiday-themed sensory bin. Use a large bin or box, and fill it with fake snow, cotton balls and/or white poms. Add in some holiday fun with jingle bells, ornaments, sparkly ribbon, white Styrofoam balls, sparkly beads, cookie cutters, etc. Allow your little one to explore the winter wonderland.

Note: Sensory bins are an inexpensive way to keep your child entertained, develop fine motor skills, experience his senses, and learn about the world. Your sensory bin can be as simple as a shallow dishpan or something on a grander scheme. Using a large plastic storage bin with a plastic table cloth underneath is a simple way to create a sensory bin, and it helps with clean-up too.

13. Sort and pattern paint cards

The most beautiful colors in cardstock…for free? Yes! Head over to your home improvement store and pick out a supply of paint color sheets. These typically have 3-4 shades per sheet.

To sort: Cut them up so that each color stands on its own. Then, dump them into a large container, and shake to mix them up. Let your toddler dump them out and sort into piles.

To pattern: Give your child a small number of color squares and help him learn to make a pattern (for example: red, yellow, red, yellow, green; red, yellow, red, yellow, green). Start simple with the patterns and let him create his own patterns as he learns. Working with patterns is the most basic beginning to mastering math skills.

14. Sticker fun

A few sheets of stickers equals hours of fun. A younger child will enjoy sticking the stickers all over a piece of paper randomly, or on themselves. An older child can learn shapes or letters by placing small stickers (like the large packs of gold stars you can get at the store) along the lines of a letter or shape that you've drawn on a piece of paper. Be extra careful with younger children – they are tempted to try eating the stickers too.

15. Matching bows

Christmas morning leaves you with a bounty of leftover bows. Gather them up and play this color matching game. First, tape up construction paper sheets to your walls in the same colors as the bows (blue, green, red, gold, etc.). Give your child a box of bows and have them sort by sticking the bows to the sheets of paper. If the sticky on your bows is gone, fold pieces of tape and stick them around the paper before the game so your tot can press the bows onto the paper with ease.

16. Explore "Soft" with cotton balls

Explore the sensation of "Soft" with cotton balls. Let your toddler pull them apart, squish them, and place them all in a big bowl. With the wintry weather outside, you can also make an indoor snowman with your cotton balls by gluing them onto a piece of paper.

17. Thread pipe cleaners through a colander

This activity is simple, mesmerizing and great for chilly days indoors. Give your toddler a handful of colorful pipe cleaners and a colander. Show him how to stick the pipe cleaners through the holes, like little worms poking through the ground.

18. Write a letter to Santa

Modify this activity according to your beliefs and traditions. For a traditional Christmas activity, help your toddler write a letter to Santa describing his wish list. Help him draw the items as he sees them in his mind, and write the word of each item next to the drawing. Suggest saying "Hello" first and then introduce themselves. Try to make it an exercise in being polite and asking nicely. Help fold the letter, put it in an envelope and address it to Santa, decorating the envelope if he wishes. There are many options for actually delivering the letter too. Stamp it properly, and send the letter to the following address: Santa Claus; North Pole; HOH, OHO, Canada. You can also deliver the letter to a Macy's department store where they have started the tradition of leaving a large red mailbox for Santa in their stores.

19. Grow a crystal snowflake with pipe cleaners

This is an all-time favorite science experiment for toddlers! You can create a snowflake to hang on a tree or on your window. You can also create a variety of other ornaments using various colors and shapes. The result is simply magical!

Supplies: String, a jar, pipe cleaners, Borax, a pencil, boiling water, food coloring and scissors.

Instructions: Make the shape of a snowflake by cutting a pipe cleaner into three equal sections and twisting the sections together at the center. Tie string to one end of the snowflake. Tie the other end of the string around the middle of a pencil. Fill the jar with boiling water. Add Borax one tablespoon at a time to the boiling water, stirring to dissolve. Use approximately 3 tablespoons of Borax per cup of water. The end result should be water that is very murky. If desired, tint the water with food coloring. Blue is a perfect color for snowflakes. Hang the pipe cleaner into the jar by resting the pencil across the jar opening. The pipe cleaner should be completely covered with liquid and hang freely in the water. The crystals may not form correctly if the pipe cleaner touches any of the sides or bottom. If the string is too long, wrap it around the pencil until you get the desired length. Allow the jar to sit undisturbed overnight. The next day, pull up the string and your pipe cleaners will be covered in crystals! Hang your crystal snowflake on the Christmas tree or near a window to catch the sunlight. To grow crystals in other shapes, twist the pipe cleaners into any design or use cookie cutters to help you form a shape.

20. Explore Valentine's Day

Want to say Happy Valentine's Day to your little loves? Create an extraordinary sensory bin by filling a plastic container with heart-shaped message candies, pink poms, a stuffed animal, heart-shaped foam cutouts, old Valentine's Day cards, and anything else red, pink and lovely you can find! Let your toddler explore the bin until his heart's content.

Sophia Lawson

CHAPTER 3
SPRING ACTIVITIES

New life and warming weather brings the opportunity for fun activities indoors as well as fresh outside adventures.

1. Play with egg cartons and plastic eggs

For younger children, fill the eggs with items that will make various sounds when they shake it (a penny, rice, a button, etc.). Any household objects will do. Have them guess what's inside and then open the eggs to discover the item. Wash the egg carton before use to get rid of any germs.

2. Make a bird feeder

Use a toilet paper roll or pine cone, and add peanut butter and birdseed. Have your toddler smear the peanut butter on the cardboard or cone, and then roll it in bird seed. You can attach a string to either end and help him hang it over a tree. Watch the birds together as they feast on your creation. Talk about the birds you see, and help him draw a picture of his favorite bird.

3. Library and lunch

Take a trip to the library, either during a scheduled "story time" or simply allow them to browse and select a book. On the way home, stop somewhere for a picnic lunch and read the story together.

4. Make a caterpillar out of an egg carton

Your carton of eggs can have a second life as a caterpillar with this fun springtime activity. Wash your used carton thoroughly to remove any germs. Then cut it down the middle to separate into two long lines. This will be the base of your toddler's caterpillar. From here, the caterpillar is formed out of pipe cleaners, markers and your toddler's imagination. Stick two black pipe cleaners onto the head for the caterpillar's antennas. Your toddler can draw eyes and a mouth with markers, and make designs on the caterpillar's body with markers, glitter, fuzzy material, etc. Mommy can make one too! Then take your caterpillars outside to crawl around.

5. Visit a pet store

Spring brings new life, and what better way to teach this lesson than to take a fun field trip to a pet store. Let your toddler take a look at the fish, kittens, puppies, guinea pigs, amphibians, and more. Talk about everything you see.

6. Farm animal match-up and memory games

Print out pictures of animals (you can find many pictures on Google Images) and glue them to heavy cardstock. Cut each picture down the middle so that the top half of the animal's body is separated from the bottom half. Mix up the pictures, and help your child match up the "head" with the "tail". Talk about the features and the sounds the animals make.

To play a farm animal memory game, print out pictures of animals and glue to heavy cardstock or wooden squares – two of each kind of animal. Mix up the animals, line them up in several rows and spend some time looking at them. Then, turn the squares over and begin playing a memory game. To play, the player turns over one square and then turns over a second square that they believe matches the first. If it doesn't match, the player's turn ends. If it does match, the player removes the two squares and places them in his or her lap. At the end, count up how many squares each player has to determine who has the most. This game works well for toddlers about two years of age and up. You will be surprised to see how quickly your young child strengthens his memory!

7. Play the I-spy bottle game

Take a 2-liter bottle and cut off the top. Fill it with a few small, brightly-colored objects and a few harder to find objects (like a thimble or paper clip). Fill up the bottle with bird seed to cover up the items. Securely tape the top back on and shake. Then, make a list of the items for your toddler to find. Have him turn and shake the bottle until he finds an item, and put a big check mark next to the items he finds on the list.

8. Make a St. Patrick's Day sensory bin with Jell-O®

Have your toddler help you make green Jell-O. Later, fill a bin with the chilled Jell-O and cookie cutters, green poms, green pipe cleaners, measuring cups, foam shamrock shapes, and anything else St. Patrick's Day inspired. Jell-O is a fantastic sensory experience for young children, and as an edible treat it's mom-friendly too.

9. Using tongs transfer

This game helps strengthen your child's mind and motor skills. Give them child-friendly tongs and items to transfer. Poms are perfect for this, though marbles would work as well. Give your child a clean egg carton and have them transfer the items one-by-one using the tongs, sorting by color into the carton compartments.

10. Go to a park and feed the ducks

Expand your toddler's world and satisfy their curiosity with a trip to a local park/pond. Talk about everything you see – the trees, the birds, butterflies, dogs, kids, grass, the sky, the shapes of the clouds, the feel of the air and the breeze, leaves, flowers, and more. Talk about the colors, shapes, and textures. This is a wonderful opportunity to boost your toddler's communication skills. End the outing with a treat – feeding the ducks! Encourage your toddler to pick out his favorite duck and give it a name. Later on, help your toddler draw a picture of his duck and end the day with show-and-tell with Daddy.

11. Toss bean-bags into a bucket

This is a simple game, whether you want to play along with your toddler or set up the game for solo play. Give your child 4 to 5 bean bags and a large bucket. Have him stand a small distance away, and toss the bean bags into the bucket. Don't have bean bags? It's easy to make your own. Cut out two squares of fabric. Place together, and hot glue three of the sides along the seam. Fill with dried beans. Close up the top by hot gluing the final seam.

12. Write a springtime book

Encourage your little author in the making. Staple a few sheets of white paper together and draw and color together to create a story about spring. Or, base your story off anything your child wants – let his imagination run wild. You can also use magazines. Help your toddler select and cut pictures out, and then glue them to form pictures in the book.

13. Make a pillow pile to jump on

Go on a search around the house for pillows. Work together to make a pile of pillows in the middle of the room. Have your toddler get a running start, and then jump into the middle…over and over again! Make sure you keep your pillow pit clear of any hard or pointy surfaces that could cause a nasty bump.

14. Talk on a cup telephone

Get two plastic cups. Poke a hole in the bottom of each cup and stick a string through it, tying the string to a paper clip inside the cups at each end so that the string doesn't come loose. Then, pull the string taut and play telephone. Practice telling each other secrets, or guessing the special word. Talk about how special our voices are, and how they are so powerful they can travel across the room.

15. Play with Velcro

Toddlers love Velcro. They love the way it sticks, the sound it makes as it pulls apart, feeling its scratchy side, and more. This activity will appeal to their senses and help them develop their fine motor skills. First, take a shoebox and hot glue squares of Velcro onto it. Then, take any item you think your toddler will enjoy sticking to the box and tape or glue the other side of the Velcro to it. Allow your toddler to stick the items to the box, and see him smile with joy as the Velcro rips away.

16. Explore "Crunchy" with eggs

Eggs are such a fun thing to explore for a toddler – the shells are smooth, then they crack. Take extra care that your child doesn't eat the shells or hurt his finger. Crack several eggs and let the insides drain out – then wash the shells to make sure you've taken care of any germs. Put the shells into a large bowl. Try to leave a few of the shells mostly intact. A great way to do this is to poke a hole into each end of the egg and blow out the insides so that the shell isn't cracked in half. Your child will love to opportunity to explore the crunchy shells!

17. Play the "Grab Bag and Guess" game

Fill a large bag (paper or gift bag) with an assortment of items varying in shape, size and texture. Here are a few ideas: toilet paper roll, apple, stuffed animal, feather, shoelace, button, paintbrush and toy. Have your toddler place his hand in the grab bag – either instructed not to look, or with something placed over his eyes. Then, let him take a guess at what he has grabbed. Pull out the item and show excitement over his correct guess; or if he has guessed incorrectly tell him "great try!" and talk about features of the object that can help him guess correctly next time.

18. Have an impromptu egg hunt

Break out the colorful plastic eggs again after Easter and have an impromptu egg hunt. Fill the objects with little "surprises," like a jelly bean, piece of apple, sticker, button, etc. Hide the eggs quickly during your child's nap. Later, head outside for a fun egg hunt. This is also a great activity for rainy days – just hold the hunt inside.

19. Make a nature bracelet

Create nature bracelets with a bit of tape and anything beautiful and interesting you can find outside. Here's what you'll need: Duct Tape. Yes, that's it! These days Duct Tape comes in a wide variety of colors and patterns, even animal print. Tear off a piece of tape large enough to fit around your child's wrist. Turn the tape sticky-side-out and wrap around his wrist. Encourage your little one to stick various items you find outside onto his bracelet to fill it up.

20. Learn about body features with a Zip-Bag book

Zip-Bag books are a wonderful way to create customized stories for your child. Once you make the "book" you can insert new photos to create entirely new stories, like learning shapes for example. In this version, make each page a close-up of your child's various body features. Toddlers love seeing their own picture or reflection.

Here's what you'll need:

- Ziploc® bags (about five bags per book);

- tape;

- pictures of your child's eyes, nose, mouth, ear, arm, hand, leg, feet, and a full body shot;

- double-sided paper (like scrapbook paper);

- a strip of fabric about 4 inches wide and as long as your bag;

- and your method for attaching the fabric – either sewing or hot glue.

First, place two bags on top of each other and use a small amount of tape to secure them together. Add each bag individually, taping each on top of the others as you go.

Once you have all five taped together, add a longer piece of tape along the spine just to secure.

Cut your piece of scrap fabric the same length as the bag. Fold it over the spine, pin it, and sew a seam straight down. Or, use hot glue to hold it all together.

Now, mount your pictures on a paper cut slightly smaller than 6"x6"; adjust the size of your paper as needed to make it fit within your seamed bag. Finally, once all your pictures are mounted and you've written in any text you'd like, slip the pages inside and "zip" them shut. Ta-da! You've made a custom body features book to read with your toddler.

Note that this is an activity the parent creates before hand and then uses during play time with the toddler. The making of this book may not be a safe activity to conduct with your toddler; but they will love the finished product!

Sophia Lawson

CHAPTER 4

SUMMER ACTIVITIES

Late days and warm weather creates the opportunity to maximize the outdoors and get a little wet and messy in the process.

1. Paint with anything but a paintbrush

Encourage your toddler to get creative and think outside the box. In this activity, your toddler will paint a picture with anything BUT a paintbrush. Items like toy cars, feathers, plastic animals, and halved potatoes make great painting utensils. Sponges also make a great painting tool – cut a household sponge into a few smaller pieces (squares or shapes), soak them in color and let your toddler smear and stamp. Give him a large piece of paper, a few colors of thick paint, and let him explore the shapes and textures that come from everyday items. This may get messy, so go outside and enjoy the nice weather while painting.

2. Water pouring

Grab a variety of containers from your kitchen or recycle bin: old apple juice jugs, measuring cups, plastic bowls, etc. Mix a bucket full of bubbly water (using dish soap or bubble bath). Place the containers outside with the water, and let your toddler use cups to pour the water in and out of the various containers. Add a few drops of food coloring for extra fun! Have a towel and change of clothes handy, because they will get wet.

3. Sidewalk art

Draw a picture together outside using sidewalk chalk. Need some inspiration? Have your tot lie down and draw an outline of his body, and then let him "decorate" his outline with eyes, nose, hair, clothes, and more.

4. Play with suds

Suds are so much fun for toddlers, and remarkably mess-free for moms. Before you start dinner, pour dish soap into your sink or a bowl and use your sprayer to spray water into the sink to create plenty of suds. Scoop the suds off the top of the water and place just the suds into a big bowl. Give the bowl to your child with a spoon and some cups, and he'll explore the sensation of the suds while you cook.

5. Plant something green

Early summer is a great time to plant something with your toddler. Let them select a flower at the store and find an appropriate place to plant it. Give them safe gardening tools to use and let them help you dig and place the flower in the ground. Let them use a small water can (or make your own out of a jug) to water the plant. This is an activity that can be revisited throughout the season, as they help you water their own special plant and watch it grow.

6. Blow bubbles

Giant-sized or small bubbles are a great activity for outdoor fun! There are many options today, from scented and colored bubbles to small machines that churn out a fountain of bubbles. Or, there's always dish soap and an old bubble wand!

7. Write letters to family members

Your toddler may be too young to write, but they can convey their messages with pictures and a ton of stickers. Help them put their "letter" in an envelope and put a stamp on it. Take a trip to the mailbox - or post office for extra fun - and make a big deal out of them putting the letter in the box. You can also include a stamped return envelope so that the recipient can easily return a letter to your tot. They will be so excited to get a letter in the mail!

8. Make fruity popsicles

Plastic popsicle sets are sold in many stores, and are a great way to make homemade and healthy popsicles during the hot days of summer. If you don't have a set, you can always use Dixie® cups and popsicle sticks. Have your toddler help you make fruity popsicles by pouring juice or Kool-Aid into the cups. Then, have your toddler drop small pieces of chopped fruit into the cups. Place a popsicle stick in each cup and let it freeze.

9. Use your noodle

This game utilizes the long foam noodles that inevitably make their way into your home every summer. Toddlers are mesmerized by the noodle – it's colorful, soft and you can swing it around. If you want to take noodle fun one step further, make a game by blowing up balloons and hitting them with the noodle stick. For more advanced fun, get a large box and encourage your little one to bat the balloons into the box. Ask him to show you how many balloons he can get into the box.

10. Explore the ocean...right at home

To create this ocean sensory experience, use a large plastic storage bin and fill it with aquarium rocks, aquarium plants, glass-colored rocks, sea shells, etc. Start the sensory experience without water, and let your little one pour the water in to see how the objects look and feel "under the sea".

11. Put together a popsicle stick puzzle

Kids eat a lot of popsicles in the summer...and so do moms! Collect 4 to 5 sticks, and then make your own puzzle. Take a picture and cut it into strips that match the size of your popsicle sticks. Glue the picture strips onto the sticks until each stick creates a piece of the puzzle. Put the sticks into a plastic bag and shake it up. Your toddler can then arrange the sticks so that it re-creates the image. This is so easy, cheap and a great activity to pack in your purse to keep your toddler busy and entertained on the go.

12. Paint the house

Using a bucket filled with water and a paintbrush, head outside with your toddler and let him pretend to "paint" your house with the water.

13. Get messy in a kiddy pool

Take your plastic kiddy pool outside and give your toddler finger paints and spray bottles filled with water tinted with a drop of food coloring. Messy fun will ensue, but clean-up is easy with a hose.

14. Catch a firefly

When twilight begins to fall, head outside with a bug catcher or jar. Because fireflies move so slowly and often land right on your hand, catching a firefly is actually possible for an older toddler. Younger toddlers will need your assistance. Watch the fireflies glow in the jar. At the end of the evening, allow your toddler to set them free to rejoin their firefly families.

15. Construct a camera and go on a safari

If you don't have a play camera on hand, your toddler can easily make his own with just about any object and a few markers. Set out on a safari, and have your toddler take imaginary pictures of the animals (or wildlife) he sees. Go inside and "develop" a picture by drawing on a piece of paper.

16. Hold a book parade

When reading in a chair just won't do, line up your favorite books in a book parade. Choose a room, or several, and place your books along a parade path. Then, start the parade with a bit of Pomp and Circumstance as you march from book to book reading the stories.

17. Play Red-Light-Green-Light to learn "Stop" and "Go"

Teach your toddler whatever version of Red-Light-Green-Light he can manage. Color paper plates red or green and hold them up to further emphasize "Stop" and "Go". Have your toddler stand on one side of the room or yard, and when you yell "Green!" he can run toward you. When you yell "Red!" he has to freeze. You may also need to add "Stop" and "Go" in your verbal directions. If your toddler is too young to master this on his own, hold his hand and run along with him as you shout the commands.

18. Plastic cup bowling

Plastic cups become "pins" and any ball will do. Your toddler can help you stack the cups on top of each other to make a pyramid. Then, have him step back and roll a small ball toward the cups to knock them down.

19. Call Grandma and Grandpa

Beef up your toddler's communication skills and help them bond with their family or friends too. Take some time to ring up Grandpa and Grandma, or have a play date with a far-away cousin. Get a little high-tech and Skype instead of using a phone. A web-cam can be purchased from Amazon or a big box/electronics store for under $50, and an online Skype (www.skype.com) account is free of charge. Dial someone via Skype and you can see them on the computer as you chat.

20. Picture-clue scavenger hunt

Though your toddler may not be able to read, he can still follow clues! Create a scavenger hunt where pictures serve as the clues. This game will exercise your toddler's brain and body as he recognizes the item, remembers where it is in the house, and scurries off to find it.

Instructions: Take pictures of about 10 items around your house. Lay out the game by attaching the clues to the objects. Start the hunt by giving your toddler a box that holds a picture of the first clue inside (for example, a teddy bear). When he finds the teddy bear in his room, the next picture will be attached (for example, a potted plant). When he finds the plant, the next clue is attached, and on it goes! The final clue leads to a location of a prize, which could be an edible treat, new toy, or even just a special activity like watching a favorite video with some popcorn or an impromptu swim in his kiddy pool.

Sophia Lawson

CHAPTER 5

FALL ACTIVITIES

Beautiful colors, crisp weather, and fun food and festivities make this season a prime time for creativity and exploration.

1. Bean sorting

Your grocery store is full of bulk bags of dried beans. Get a large amount of dried beans and dump them into a large container. Break out other spoons, cups and sorting utensils. Let your little one go to work on sorting the beans, and encourage them with words that describe more, less, empty, in, out, smooth, scratchy, etc. Supervise extra closely with this activity, as dried beans can be a big choking hazard for young toddlers.

2. Pumpkin hunt game

It's time to go on a pumpkin hunt! Prepare the game by cutting out pumpkin shapes with orange construction paper, writing the numbers 1 – 10, and putting a bit of tape on the back of each pumpkin. Stick the pumpkins at various places around your house or yard. Send your toddler on a pumpkin hunt to gather all 10 pumpkins.

3. Fall nature box

Fall is a fantastic time to explore nature with vibrant colors and textures. Grab a large tub or box and fill it with all sorts of interesting things from the outside: pine needles, pine cones, foliage of all colors, dried leaves and twigs, as well as a few other surprises like a toilet paper roll, small gourds, etc. Let your toddler search the box and explore the sensory experience of fall.

4. Bake something, like an apple treat

Allowing your toddler to help you cook is so much fun. For this easy and healthy treat, preheat the oven to 375°F. Core the apples leaving the bottom closed, and peel the top half of the apple. Fill the apple with dried or frozen cranberries. Top off the apple with brown sugar, a bit of butter and sprinkle with cinnamon. Bake the apple(s) for 35-45 minutes, until they are soft. Enjoy the treat with your toddler after lunch!

Another extremely fun activity for toddlers, although less healthy, is to decorate iced cookies. For quick cooking, use premade sugar cookie dough from your grocery store and cut into circles (or roll it out and cut into shapes). Put a very thin amount of icing on the cookie and give your toddler a few edible sprinkles and decorations. Some children will wildly shake sprinkles on the cookies, while others painstakingly decorate with each dot. If you don't want a dozen cookies lying around the house, put the nicest ones one a plate and go with your toddler to deliver them to a neighbor, teaching generosity as well.

5. Build a fort and watch a movie in it

When the days get extra chilly, stay warm and cozy inside your house with this special treat. First, build a fort in your house with your toddler – make it large enough for everyone to fit inside comfortably. Pop some popcorn and snuggle up inside to watch your toddler's favorite "movie" (or shorter video for smaller attention spans).

6. Glow in the dark bath time

It starts getting dark much earlier in the fall. So what better way to bring some excitement to your toddler's bath than to add a few glow sticks! Glow sticks can be bought at most dollar stores. You just snap and place the sticks in the water or around your child like a necklace or bracelet. Put the sticks in the freezer after the bath, and they will last a second day.

7. Make handprint art

Handprint art is easy, fun, and unique to every child. In this variation, make a Thanksgiving turkey. Trace your toddler's handprint on a plain piece of paper. Your child can then color in the turkey feathers, add eyes, name the turkey, and more. Construction paper and glue can also be a fun way to decorate a turkey handprint. Ideas for other holidays include a reindeer, elephants, and flowers – all using your child's handprint.

8. Put on a puppet show

Help your toddler make her very own puppets out of a paper bag or old sock. If you want to keep it simple, just flip a table and start the show. However, another fun variation is to create your own hallway puppet theater. Take a sheet, and cut a square-shaped hole in the middle; decorate with markers or other craft supplies to create a red curtain, stage, lights, etc. Tack the sheet up, and the show can take place behind the "curtain". It can be used over and over for years to come!

9. Marbles game

This easy game helps develop your toddler's fine motor skills and problem solving. Get out some marbles and a plastic soda bottle (or similar object). Younger children will enjoy just placing all the different colored marbles in the bottle with their hands, possibly lifting it up and shaking it to hear the sound. Older toddlers will enjoy a more advanced game when you incorporate a spoon. Have them lift the marble up with the spoon and transfer it into the bottle without dropping it. Keep a close eye to be sure your toddler does not put the marbles in his mouth.

10. Play dress up

Get out the Halloween costumes and any other accessories from your toddler's closet. For a special treat, let your toddler raid your closet as well. Begin playing dress up, including trying on Mom or Dad's clothes and accessories.

11. Make a meal with play dough…plus make your own dough!

Thanksgiving dinner, anyone? Break out the play dough and make a pretend supper – corn, meat, rolls, carrots, green beans, and pie for dessert. If you're concerned about your toddler eating the commercial brand dough, make your own edible dough. Here's how:

Kool-Aid Play Dough

1 cup water

1 cup flour

1/2 cup salt

1 package Kool-Aid mix or Jell-O° mix (unsweetened)

3 teaspoons Cream of Tartar

1 tablespoon cooking oil

Instructions: Mix dry ingredients together in a large saucepan. Mix the water and oil together and slowly add to the saucepan, while stirring over medium heat until the mixture thickens to form dough. Place on a heatproof service and knead until cool enough for children to handle. Dough will be colored and scented like the mix. This dough can be stored in a tightly covered container for a few months.

Peanut Butter Play Dough

18-oz. jar creamy peanut butter

6 tablespoons honey

3/4 cup non-fat dry milk

Instructions: Mix ingredients together, using varying amounts of dry milk for desired consistencies. This dough must be stored in an airtight container, and should be used within one week.

12. Draw on a gourd

Inexpensive small pumpkins or gourds can be bought at your local grocery store (or pumpkin patch) in the fall. Pick up a mini pumpkin and let your child draw a design or face. Write your child's name on the back and set it on your porch or mantle for decoration.

13. Mash potatoes

This activity provides tons of entertainment for your toddler, and he may even enjoy eating a little too! Prepare the potatoes for mashing by peeling them, cutting into smaller chunks and boiling them for 10 minutes. Once they are completely cool, place them in a bowl and give your toddler something safe he can mash them with – like a large spoon. He will undoubtedly use his hands as well.

14. Jump in the leaves

It's simple and straightforward: rake the fall leaves from your yard into a large pile (and don't forget to let your little helper assist as well). Then jump, toss and tumble in a wonderfully crispy sea of red and yellow leaves.

15. Make mummies with toilet paper

For a little Halloween fun, get a roll of toilet paper and let your toddler make a Daddy or Mommy Mummy by wrapping the paper around you…then return the favor as you wrap him too.

16. Run an obstacle course made out of cushions and/or furniture

Obstacle courses are great for kids of all ages. Simple courses can provide a magnitude of fun for your toddler. Using cushions, pillows, safe furniture and more, create a course to challenge your child to weave through tunnels, around blockades, and jump over mounds. Stack cups that he can bust through, or a "pit" of balls that he must wade through. Make it as interesting as you can, while keeping it safe and not overwhelming. For added excitement, time your child and announce that he has achieved a new record!

17. Make a car or train out of a box

Little children simply love cars. From the "vroom" of the engine to the horns that beep, the tires that turn, the passengers waving, and the bounces and the jerks of the wheel. Use a large cardboard box to help your toddler transform it into a car. This is pretend play, so talk about everything and use your noises. Pull or push the box around while your child "drives" inside. Connect two or three boxes together with rope to create a train. Your toddler can go for a ride or place stuffed animals inside the boxes and conduct the train himself. Be sure to add a soundtrack with "choo, choo," "chug-a-chug-a," and "wooo, wooo!"

18. Play hide-and-seek

Does this game ever go out of style? Absolutely not. When in doubt, play hide-and-seek. For safety, stay close to your toddler and keep this game to one to two rooms. Before the game begins, walk him around and show him a few great spots to hide – he may need some inspiration. Then, go to a corner and count to ten loudly, proclaiming "Ready or not, here I come!" Make a show out of looking for your toddler, and praise him for doing a great job hiding.

19. Wiggly worms

Cook a big pot of spaghetti. If you don't mind getting messy, add a small amount of orange, green or purple food coloring to the mix. Place the pot/bowl on the floor and let your toddler enjoy squishing the spaghetti in and out of his hands. Add a few containers to his play area so that he can practice transferring the noodles. Expect a few nibbles, and if you do decide to use food coloring take the fun outside. This activity is perfect for Halloween!

20. Cut along the line

Print out some fun lines (squiggly, dotted, etc.) on a few sheets of paper. Give your toddler safety scissors and have them cut along the lines. This activity is for older toddlers who can safely handle a pair of age-appropriate scissors.

CHAPTER 6

EXTRA FUN FOR BOYS

1. Bathtub fishing

This activity is fun for children of all ages. Be careful
when using pieces small enough for a young child to
choke on, and always closely supervise your child near
water. Fill up a bathtub with water, and add a bit of
blue food coloring for extra fun. Place toys with
magnets under the water (fish or under-the-sea theme
are perfect). Create your own "fishing pole" with any
handle/stick and string or yarn, with a magnet tied at
the end of the string to serve as the hook. Place a towel
on the floor to catch the drips, and a bowl or bucket by
the tub for the items your child "catches." Then, let's go
fish! To make it even more educational, use magnets

with letters or numbers and encourage your little fisherman to catch the items in order: 1-2-3, or A-B-C!

2. Shooting monsters

Monsters are attacking our city! It's time to take action. Start off this activity with a simple craft creating the monsters. Black and white printouts of monsters can be found online for coloring, or simply have your son draw his own monster on paper and help you cut it out. Set your monsters up around outside using whatever you can find around the house (tape them to aluminum cans, for example). Fill up a water gun and blast away!

3. Animal noises

Take small pieces of paper and draw pictures of different animals. Or, if you're not an artist, print out pictures from the computer or cut out magazine photos. Write the name of the animal on each strip as well. Place them in a bag or bucket. Let your toddler pull out a strip, and then he must act out the animal complete with what noises the animal makes.

4. Squishy art

Put paint in a large plastic storage bag. Start out with the colors somewhat separated, and let your toddler squish away. It's mess-free fun!

5. Hold a Masking Tape Derby

These days, your local big box store or home improvement store will have a large assortment of tape colors and designs. Pick one up, and the next time you're stuck indoors, create your own Masking Tape Derby with matchbox cars. Run the tape along your floors, couch, cushions, etc., and hold a race around the house on the track.

6. Hammer golf tees

This activity will entertain your toddler and teach them fine motor skills. You will need a toy hammer, golf tees and a piece of Styrofoam. Stick the golf tees into the Styrofoam just enough to stand but allowing plenty of room for hammering. Let your toddler bang away as the tees go into the foam. Supervise closely in case pieces of the foam break off and become hazards.

7. Make a spooky monster

This could be fun for Halloween, or any time you feel like doing a silly craft with your boy. You'll need a few basic craft supplies, like googily eyes, yarn, fuzzy/feathery material, and whatever else you think could make a fun monster face. Have your tot make his own monster by gluing the items onto a round paper plate. For a fun Halloween decoration, pick up a cheap (usually about $1) unfinished wooden frame from your craft store, and have your toddler decorate that instead. Once it's done, you can insert a picture of your toddler in his Halloween costume.

8. Archeological dig

Fill a plastic tray with rice and hide tiny plastic dinosaurs (often available at the dollar store) trinkets or pom balls inside. Set out a few scoopers and an empty tray next to it. In another variation, you can set a cookie cooling rack on top of the empty tray so that the rice can fall through the holes and the balls or trinkets remain on top. Then let your toddler go digging – with the scoopers or just his hands.

9. Shave with Daddy

This activity is perfect for some special father-son time. Grab some shaving cream and give your little guy a popsicle stick. Help him pretend shave just like Daddy!

10. Harry mirror faces

This is fun to do in the bathroom with whiteboard markers. Have him draw hair and a mustache on the mirror around where his face is. Then erase and start again.

CHAPTER 7

SUPER SWEET FOR GIRLS

1. Clothesline play

String up a pretend clothesline and provide a few socks, some felt clothes cut-outs, a few scarves, etc. Give your toddler a few clothespins, and she can hang up her very own wash.

2. Give baby dolls a bath

Whether they're baby dolls or action figures, sometimes toys need a bath too. Set out a small tub of water, plastic baby doll or figure, towels and soap. The area will get wet and a little messy, but fun!

3. Glitter bottle

Mix water, oil and glitter in a two-liter bottle. Shake and watch the glitter swirl. This activity is mesmerizing, and it teaches density. For older children, talk about what you see, explaining that the oil is thicker than water.

4. My very own pantry

Fill up a shelf in your pantry or one cabinet in your kitchen (or drawer) with items like safe kitchen utensils, a pot, cans of soup, or a box of macaroni. Let your toddler load and unload items into her very own pantry. For extra fun, set up a little grocery area and let her go "shopping". Have her select items from the "store" and bring them back to load into her pantry. Younger children or babies will enjoy banging around on the pots/utensils or stacking and unstacking cans. Older children can engage further with pretend play.

5. Pretty fabric pulling

This can be done with an old baby wipes case or even a used tissue box. Gather up your scraps of fabric. Small bundles of various colored scrap fabrics can also be purchased at craft stores in the sewing section. Cut into strips and tie them together at the ends so they become one continuous line of fabric. Stuff them into the box and let your toddler pull them out, discovering each new color or print as they go. At the end, she can re-stuff, and pull again.

6. Play with pretend envelopes

Take an 8.5 x 11 sheet of felt fabric and fold it over, leaving about three inches at the top of one end. Hot glue (or sew) the sides together, leaving the top open. Fold the flap over and iron it down so it creates a crease. This creates your play envelope. Decorate with other pieces of felt – add a heart stamp or address area. Write pretend letters to place inside for special friends and family…like Daddy!

7. Have a tea party

While you might not want to use your fine china, a play set or plastic tableware can be used to hold a tea party. Invite your daughter's favorite stuffed animals to the party, and serve "tea" (apple juice) and biscuits (crackers). Play dress up beforehand for a fancier affair.

8. Grab a basket and go pick flowers

Enjoy the outdoors by picking wild flowers (or weeds) out in your yard. Bring along a basket to hold them. At the end let your toddler arrange a bouquet to adorn your dinner table.

9. Make a fruit loop necklace

Take a piece of string and have your toddler string her own fruit loop necklace. Do this before an outing and she can munch on her "snack" to stay busy. You can incorporate other items too, like pretzels.

10. Pretend sew with lacing cards

Sewing is a wonderful activity for little girls to learn, so why not start early with this activity that also teaches fine motor skills. Create her base by cutting out a shape (like a heart, star or circle) from a thick piece of foam. Using a hole-puncher, punch holes around the edge (not too close) to create the holes she will "sew" in. Then, using long strands of colored, thick string, have her "lace" through the holes following the pattern you've created.

CHAPTER 8

ONE TO GROW ON

This book includes 100 inspired ideas for teaching and entertaining your toddler. Now, here's one more to grow on.

Toys are wonderful for learning and entertaining, but sometimes your toddler grows weary of the same blocks, train or doll – every day. When all else fails, break out a special box of toys as a special treat for your child. Change the contents of the box every few weeks or so depending on your child's age or interests.

One way to do this is through the use of "busy bags". You can start a collection of busy bags, which are simple and age appropriate activities grouped in plastic storage bags. They can be pulled out and easily assembled by your child when you need just a few minutes of uninterrupted time. They can also be stashed in your purse/bag while on the go so your child can be easily entertained while you are running errands, waiting at the doctor's office, watching a sibling's soccer game, etc.

The Busy Bag Swap

Busy bag ideas can be found all over the internet, but what if you are pressed for time and creativity? A Busy Bag Swap can be a great way to compile a large amount of busy bags. Get together with a group of moms (for this example, 20 moms) and hold a busy bag party. For the party, each parent creates 20 bags of the same project – a far easier task than creating 20 entirely different projects or activities. Then, you have a "party" where you swap bags, meaning you'll leave the event with 20 completely different busy bags – one from each participant. Not only is a Busy Bag Swap a great opportunity to relax and chat with fellow moms, but you'll leave with great activities for your child too!

Also By Sophia Lawson

Baby Sleep Training Made Simple: From Naps to Sleeping Through the Night

Amazon Bestseller!

Available on Amazon: http://amzn.to/PeSdH3

Do you want to train your baby to take predictable daily naps and sleep through the night? Then you'll love this book! Lawson brings you a guide to baby sleep training that's simple and easy to digest. Learn from someone who has been through ALL the troubleshooting. This bestseller includes:

- Sample Schedules to get you going TODAY
- Quick Reference Guide
- Tips for minimizing crying
- Steps tailored for starting late

Get your copy now for step-by-step instructions to implement this proven, trusted sleep training method.

Other Thrive Press Bestsellers

MONKEYS: Jungle Series – With Facts, Trivia and Photos!

By Emma Reed

Find it on Amazon now:
www.amazon.com/dp/B00BGFWOPW

Part of the Amazon Bestselling Animals Series, EXPEDITION EARTH!

Simply Stylish:

How to Revamp Your Wardrobe for Chic Style At Any Age

By D.C. Stylist Carrie Foster

Getting dressed can be fast, easy and fun when you've got simple style!

Find it on Amazon now:
www.amazon.com/dp/B00B9MAID2

PEG BOARD

Write Your Own Ideas and Notes Here!

_____
_____
_____
_____
_____
_____
_____
_____
_____
_____
_____
_____
_____
_____
_____
_____
_____
_____
_____

_____

_____

_____

_____

_____

_____

_____

_____

_____

_____

_____

_____

_____

_____

_____

_____

_____

_____

_____

_____

_____

_____

About the Author

Sophia Lawson is an acclaimed writer and editor, published in magazines and journals worldwide. Lawson specializes in child development and technology, and is known affectionately as the "Babywise Mom". Her greatest achievement, however, is being a mother and wife. Lawson lives outside of Atlanta, Ga., and while not working she enjoys crafting with her daughter, yoga, outdoor adventures, and reading a good book under her favorite magnolia tree.